ENDORSEMENTS

Before I comment on the book from a professional perspective of an accredited BACP counsellor in private practice, I feel it is important to give an insight into the author.

I first met Ellie on a gloriously sunny evening in Harthill, a small village in Yorkshire, England. I had been looking for a meditation group for self-care purposes but could not find one that would fit into my busy schedule. I couldn't believe that there was one advertised within walking distance and on an evening that I was work free!

Ellie was leading this group. Her energy hit me as soon as I walked in the room. She was very welcoming, efficient and had an air of confidence. I was intrigued to know more about this person and how this effervescent lady would hold a meditation group.

I thoroughly enjoyed the sessions and felt a growing connection with Ellie, we had shared symmetry through previous working lives, living abroad and a wicked sense of humour. Ellie became a good friend and confidante in a small group of sisters that have been invaluable, especially in these challenging times.

When I first read the draft copy of Ellie's book I was so struck by its honesty and deep outpourings on a personal note. I was then impressed as a counsellor, as to how this book could play a pivotal part in self-expression and care. I encourage my clients to use a journal; to check in with their feelings, to capture difficult situations, to rant, to rejoice and to map out their journey to recovery.

A journal is testament to what we have experienced and to how we have dealt with difficulties. We can then revisit it to remind us how far we have come. I feel 'Shadow Time' could be a catalyst for expressing emotional freedom.

Amanda France MBACP (Accred.)
Amanda@afcounselling.co.uk

The first time I met Ellie, she was in my reflexology chair. She had been overly busy, and life had been somewhat cruel lately; her body was telling her to slow down. So, she listened, and opted for putting better self-care in place. But her mind never stood still – far too many ideas!

For her new home, for her business, and how to create a positive impact within the community.

She was a math and English teacher and a holistic therapist. She's a wife, mother, and grandmother. She's a creator and runs her own businesses. If she sets her mind to something, she will make it work.

But above all, she is a friend. She has helped me on my way many times. Beautiful, direct, sharing, caring, kind and compassionate. Fun-loving.

In this book, Ellie shares some of her personality with us. She lets the poetry reflect her own true brilliance – as she experiences, captures, and lives life.

Femke A. Williams
www.feetupforever.co.uk

I had the pleasure meeting the enigmatic force that is Ellie, a few years ago. She came along, with some friends, to a painting workshop I was delivering at my Vintage Arts and Crafts Centre in Worksop, North Notts.

I was immediately struck with how vibrant and jovial she was, and I thoroughly enjoyed her participation, inquisitive nature and creations from that day.

Whilst chatting between the schedule, Ellie invited me to join her new ladies business networking group and I was delighted to accept. I mean, who wouldn't accept the occasional evening of child-free socialising with fine dining, drinks and grown-up chat?

Greeted like a best friend on my first attendance, I was grateful to find what felt like a fresh tribe to mingle with and I hoped to make some positive connections.

From that day on, Ellie has evolved to be a much loved and appreciated spirit in my life. With an elusive balance of humour, frankness, and genuine empathy, I don't think twice in sharing my most crazy, funny or sad moments with her, as I know it will be met as it was intended to be received.

I will also never let her forget the night she drove myself and a handful of friends to the middle of nowhere for a shopping social event. That was the best and worst night out I have ever had! The kind where your stomach muscles hurt from laughing, and whilst avoiding any eye contact with anyone, you politely step over a grown man lying on the floor when you leave and remain silent, until safely locked inside the car and on the journey home!

Ellie has a wicked talent for mixing cocktails, making chutney, which (along with a spoon and some crackers) has got me through some sad and frumpy days, when I've happily wrapped myself up with a blanket on the sofa and enjoyed her food hug in a jar.

She emits a wealth of positivity and creativity, which comes to fruition in many ways, including up-cycling, home interiors and helping others achieve their goals.

When Ellie shared with me that she was writing a poetry book, I was genuinely intrigued. Similar to myself, she's a cat who has enjoyed at least 7 of her 9 lives, in her depth of perception and experiences.

Curled up in my comfy spot at home, glass of fizz to hand, I read through the transcript. Like the introduction warns, there are poems that invite you to get involved, that resonate, make you giggle or nod along knowingly, alongside some that have a darker shade or may simply make you raise an eyebrow.

I hope that bringing together and encapsulating a lifetime of thoughts, emotions and whims between these pages, will also allow you, Ellie, to draw with your beautifully manicured claws, a line in the snow and look ahead to new beginnings. Bravo Lady xx

Helen Parry
Carlton House Vintage, Art & Craft Centre, Worksop
hcpaz@me.com

DEDICATED TO...

My darling daughter, Rachel. The best work I've ever produced.

'Per Ardua ad Astra'

PREFACE

I have a framed print on my office windowsill that I catch sight of every single day. It shows a weedy, be-speckled chap rowing oar onboard a rowing boat, shackled to other poor unfortunates overseen by a burly thug with a whip in his hand.

Above the image reads:

"Mind you, this job isn't so bad – I used to be a teacher!"

It makes me chuckle and reminisce about my teaching days in state schools in the UK. I'm reminded about teaching English classes and in particular Shakespearian comedy to a class of disaffected fourteen-year-olds.

Trying to explain that, to Shakespeare's Elizabethan audience, cross-dressing was hilarious. Young boys pretending to be girls, girls pretending to be boys was pant-wettingly funny and would of guaranteed The Bard a full house at The Globe Theatre in old London, no doubt!

"But it ain't funny Miss!"

Quite. What constituted 'funny' may have substantially changed over 500 years and I felt like a comedian dying on stage when delivering my lessons. I was never a career teacher. Far from it, I'd already climbed the greasy pole out in the Construction industry before I had the bright idea that I'd like to give back my life experiences to date and teach. Mistakenly thinking, I had some sort of "vocation". In hindsight, the real appeal (if I'm honest) was that as a single mum at the time, the holidays were great.

It did, however, give me the opportunity to read and study some marvellous classic and contemporary literature and appraise my mother tongue.

My appreciation of poetry grew into a love-affair with the crafted word on the page. My middle-aged rantings several years ago have mellowed over time. I recently re-discovered a tatty but bulging old journal; Its contents were held in place with an old rubber band.

Inside were my scribblings from fifteen years ago. For a short while, I used to enter Slam-poetry competitions, partly for the challenge and partly because I was single at the time and able to flirt with sexy poets. I remember that period of time in my life as fun, exciting and fulfilling a need to express myself.

My personal style or "voice" as a poet has evolved over the years as you'd expect after writing several thousand words drawn from my febrile imagination. I especially liked to hear my words spoken, which is why I attended the "Slams".

However, you'd expect a trained teacher, used to striding into a classroom of teenagers, showing no stage fright at these events.

"They can sense fear on you darling and will rip you to shreds, don't smile at the little shits till Christmas."

This was the sage advice given to me on my first teaching post from the Head of English.

It wasn't true; Speaking in front of your peers is always more stressful than teenagers in the classroom. I often got a very tight voice, sounding on occasions like Minnie-Mouse. I felt dangerously exposed and judged.

In competitions, I was. I never won any prizes, only notoriety at one event for using a bad pejorative swear-word. The judges were stoney-faced after the audible gasp went up from the audience. I loved getting the reaction and my colleagues stood up and clapped.

Maybe this was what a Shakespearian actor felt like after all!

I've also considered myself an 'accidental poet' if such a creation exists. We are often advised that if you want to consider yourself a writer, well, you fundamentally have to pick up your pen (or tap away at a keyboard) and connect the imagination to the page.

Writing takes verve and a strong will to discipline yourself to devote time away from your daily activities. It's far too easy to procrastinate and put off the actual act of writing. I'm a busy businesswoman and it's far too easy to sack-off the writing for yet another networking event or LinkedIn Zoom call.

I decided to write as a way of coping with the Lockdown situations because of the Covid-19 pandemic in the UK from Spring 2020. There was only so much housework, jigsaw puzzles and walks to the little parade of shops in my village I could take before the pull of yet another Netflix TV box set lured me like a siren onto my sofa.

My mental health was supported by journaling my daily thoughts. There was a progressive journey of emotion, like experiencing grief. Indeed, I felt the familiar aching void of shock, disbelief, anger then a grudging acceptance and gradual adaptation to the "new normal" way of doing business and interacting with friends on "Zoom" calls. It had lighter moments, training my 84-year-old mother to make a FaceTime call on her new phone was hilarious.

Several minutes of looking up my mum's nose and the ceiling before she got the hang of it!

It was at once nostalgic and a revelation, reviewing and drafting work on some poems that I first wrote 15 years ago. Life had flown under several bridges, and I felt some of the lines needed re-working. It taught me that writing is as much a craft as it is art. The crafting of words is fun, painful at times but ultimately, it captured the essence of what I wanted to say.

Dear Reader, I hope that this compilation of poetry helps you explore and celebrate all the flavours of your life from the dark and macabre to the whimsical and light. I've given you space by adding a bonus journal section for you to document the flavours of your life too.

Enjoy the process!

Ellie

TABLE OF CONTENTS

INTRODUCTION

Understanding the quiet, shadow side of ourselves is never easy. During testing times, take inspiration from the animal spirit totem of the Snow Leopard.

When your mind is getting fatigued by all the external and internal 'noise', take time to recharge your energy. The Snow Leopard reminds you that you alone have the power to change yourself and go where no one else does, into your mind.

The Snow Leopard is a solitary creature. Journaling is a solitary activity. The 'Shadow Time' is time just for you to journal your thoughts, experiences of daily life, previous memories, positive mantras or your Mum's favourite family recipes!

Why have I added my poetry to a journal?

I've been writing poetry for years, on and off, as a personal 'safety valve' for downloading my emotions onto a page. For trying to make sense of events, observations, relationships and various adventures. Frankly, it's saved me a small fortune in therapy.

Documenting the full gamut of human emotions in an anthology of poetry is a tough task. The subtlety of emotions such as sorrow, grief or fury could lend themselves to a separate anthology. So, the themes collected here are not exhaustive, but a few signposts, to shed illumination and comment on some that I have personally experienced.

"Poetry is the shadow cast by our streetlight imagination."

(Lawrence Ferlinghetti)

Freeform Poetry, what is that?

I've always preferred Freeform – a more modern, free-wheeling tumble of language and lack of punctuation. I could explain that each word is crafted, selected to carry the weight of meaning quickly and efficiently, which it is. However, if I'm being truthful, it's appealing because it's quick and I don't have to faff about with the punctuation rules.

The line breaks help with meaning and pausing for breath and really focuses the eye on certain words for effect.

Poetry, I feel, is the author's soul on a page and as such, our vulnerabilities are exposed. The writing is designed, filtered and distilled to get to the heart of the story-telling or emotion; like a fine malt whisky sipped slowly. It's artisanal and a mature process of reflection.

I have been attracted to the American Beat Poet, Lawrence Ferlinghetti, for many years, since his work appeared on the A' Level English syllabus I had to teach. He belonged to a collective of Mid-20th century writers who, post WWII started to push the artistic frontiers of writing. They wanted to break free of the rigid constraints and shackles of conventional poetry with its strict rhyming patterns and meter. They wanted to voice their thoughts in new and sometimes shocking ways.

The lexis or meaning and onomatopoeic sound of the words becomes more important than the physical structure of rhyme.

The loose assonance (half rhyme) is used to carry the momentum through the verse.

One of the best explanations of this poetic device is highlighted in a scene from Willy Russell's play 'Educating Rita'. This was filmed in the 1980's and there is a scene where a new 'mature' student, Rita, is asked by her university professor, Frank, to explain what the word assonance means:

"Assonance, is gettin' the rhyme wrong Frank!"

What makes this journal so unique is the way I've used poetry and the illustrations to stimulate your senses and creativity.

The journal is divided into two parts; The first section is devoted to poetry exploring the themes of darkness and light. It's a jumble of mixed themes to mirror how life can really be an undulating journey.

For most people, life is a series of highlights of deep emotions, high and low, strung together with periods of calm and routine. Knowing that, whatever state you're in presently, it will not last.

The wonderful double page illustration is by my friend and accomplished artist, Sally Brown. This effectively divides the journal.

Finally, the second section is left blank for you to journal your own words and creativity.

PART 1
Poems Of Darkness & Light

"And the darkness of our bedroom is soon full of the fallen shadows of our failures."

William Gass

"To shine your brightest light is to be who you truly are."

Roy T. Bennett

How can we express those doleful feelings and hidden emotions?

Over the years, I've realised I can mine a rich, deep vein of venom and moroseness when I've been crossed in love or in business.

I've learnt that writing words on paper has been easier for me than full throttle confrontation after turmoil or relationship breakdowns. For me, it's now a form of self-care and healing.

The nights I have lain in bed, plotting my little domestic acts of revenge – tire kicking, paint splattering, plant pot smashing, suit slashing mayhem – as a way of releasing feelings of tension and disempowerment. Pretty tame in reality; just enough violence to feel some relief.

Outwardly, I'd shrug off petty insults and slights and tell my family I was "fine".

Has any other word in the English language so under-rated, and mis-used the true feeling of hurt, that the average Brit can express? "Fine thanks" can mean anything but fine!

It's all about the tone of voice. My daughter was always fond of telling me it was the *way* I was telling her off for not clearing up her messy teenage bedroom:

"Fine! It's your TONE again Mum, that TONE!... Ugh I hate that!"

The darker themed poems have tried to cover a range of emotions and situations. evilness, mysteriousness, horror, fury, heartbreak, sadness and loss.

My best advice for getting through the rotten times in life is to imagine what you would say in a scenario where you confront the hurtful situation and write down the imaginary conversation.in your journal.

Finally, let your pen be mightier than a prison sentence and get that angst out of your head, off your chest and onto the page. Either rip the page out and burn it or bury it.

Then, go and forgive yourself and them.

Literally, start a new fresh page of lighter thoughts. What joy to laugh, be silly, childish, to enjoy friendships and fall in love.

If we are lucky to have supportive families, dear trusted friends, kind and engaging networks or a pet to hug, we are, I think, going to experience a more meaningful life.

So, daydream of a happier, funnier time. Dare to hope. Dare to imagine a less stressful, sombre existence. Let grief never be forgotten but fade into the background fabric of your continuing life.

If you've newly emerged from the wreckage of a broken heart, blinking into a brighter, sunnier life like a mole poking up through the soil, blinded by too much light. Take heart. You are going to laugh your socks off one day at some tomfoolery or slapstick antics on TikTok.

It will super-charge your energy to face the day and make you feel a little lighter. Looking at the most mundane situations as well as, how absurd and frivolous moments can switch our moods, is a wonder.

Life is beautiful, messy and precious if we blink away the tears so we can see the true sparkly brilliance of it.

A Dish Best Served Korma

Based on a true-life event. I had my revenge with an ex after he betrayed me with a girlfriend of mine. I had a dinner party and served them both a portion of curry made with canned dogfood.

What's the saying...? "A woman scorned shouldn't make curry?"

A Dish Best Served Korma
Revenge

The Bard he did say
revenge is a dish best served cold
I disagree
it is a dish best served korma

Let me enlighten you

Once a friend to me
at University
good-fellowship
she did profess
unbeknown
she wormed
her way
into my
beloved's affections
bore a hole
into his heart
with her
masquerade of love
they did betray me
disrespect and disobey me
I kept the peace
quiet in the face
of their cruelty and caprice

My chance to right their
wrongs
came through

dinner opportunities
with strongly flavoured korma
my best efforts did I procure
for my guests
a beef korma with pakora
for the hellish couple
(I shouldn't tell but what the hell)
oh so tender
is the meat on her plate
a portion so lovingly catered
from dog food
tin-canned
doggie-chow-wow

This couple did
wolf down this
lip-smacking delish dish
so tender so soft
the recipe
departing so late
this despicable couple
flushed through the rot
bottoms burning
with brands of
doggie choice cuts
I got to feel
all's fair in the end
with the curry
loving c**ts

9

Peppermint Tea

Bodily functions blamed on the family pet...they had the last laugh!

Peppermint Tea
Funny

It's 6am
our spaniel yawns and pads
softly scratches the door
and whines
his needs
override mine
he escapes effortlessly outside

I'm trapped in
bleary ablution
tea and toast
the usual solution

Bubbles swirling inside me
wrapped in fleece

I sit like a bloated
furry animal
the dog nestles
sensing
kinship
I sip peppermint tea
in lady-like fashion
with the curly-haired hound
on my knees

A malodorous
whiff
wafts
I keep sipping
and blame the dog
he raises a paw
to his nose
accusingly

Abandoned by my
hairy conspirator
vanishing like
Houdini
I sit virtuously

Seeking revenge
my noble pet
defecates
on the herb patch

I drink more tea
Enigmatically

Limbs of Leylandii

Inspiration from the opening scenes of David Lean's production of Charles Dickens' classic novel 'Great Expectations'.

Imagining the limbs of a tree like hands, ready to grab!

Limbs of Leylandii
Sinister/horror

In desolate dark
churchyards
lichen-laden
headstones
mark your
place
Could find you
on a map
of orderly
death rows
plotted and paid for
with your
Co-Op
Plan

Very good at organising
your final resting
weren't you
pity
you didn't
work out the
cost
to the
family's funeral
debt

every time I walk
the dog
he repays
the interest
in piss

The skeletal
limbs of Leylandii
grab down
as if to pitch
us down to join you
I visit to chat
to mutter
that you were
a silly arse
in life
now a tight-fisted
comfy corpse

Your orderly plot
contrasts with the
home wreckage
Hope it's comfortable
on the
burning coals

May Queen

It was a shocking revelation to find out that during pagan times, there was a suggestion that the 'May Queen' may have been sacrificed in ancient fertility rituals...the blood of a fair virgin spilled over soil!

May Queen
Sinister

The May crown
lay torn
imperfect ring
on innocent
whore heads

Did she think
she wouldn't
be found
in thickets
of green

But YOU knew where
she lay
the girl-woman
who stayed
too close
to watch
your dirty secrets

the birdwatching
hides
mourn
the spectacle of
human horse play
and carnival cavorting
so you
silenced her
she'll not gossip
instead
she's making friends
with the
worms
There's a new
vacancy for
May Queen
only true
innocents apply

Perils of Kissing Wine-Knights

I just fell in love with the word wine-knight (to drink valiantly) and imagined how some slightly gone-to-seed men think they're such a catch to others!

Perils of Kissing Wine-Knights
Wry Observations

It's a sweeping generalisation
but I've found it to be true
certainly of my generation
that when kissing wine-knights
one has to be aware of
finding sage and onion
in teeth
forage about in the beards
and you can find it there too

Frankly these men deserve
to be matched with
leery ladies
sweaty-Bettys
and matrons of malice

Grooming is a dirty word
to these gloomy delectable
specimens
oh please share your
paunch
nose dribblings
and toxic bottom emissions
dignity insists
on fresh sheets
no tie-dye patterns on shrouds
with bodily fluids
laundry notwithstanding
adventuring with these valiants
can be perilous and grubbily
forsaken

If 007 was A Librarian

I was set a challenge by a published poet, that I couldn't write a piece about mashing the idea of master spy 007 and the local librarian...challenge accepted!

If 007 Was A Librarian
Whimsical

Vellum elegant
thumbed not turned
concealed
a license to shush

Dewey classification
007
if you accept the
assignments
the role involves
Top Secret
assignations
between pressed paper
character assassinations

Watermarked
typeface
cryptic classifications
stealthy caches
of fictions between
nations

If 007 was
a librarian
they would learn to
silence
with a killer title
slay
authors with
autocratic
rebuke

Scent of Meat

Imagining a mythical, dark creature being let loose in a forest...a cross between a Werewolf and the Green Man. Tapping into primordial fears of the forest.

Scent of Meat
Horror

The raw dripping pool
creeping across the
mouth
delicious

Drip drip dribble dribble

No sanguine snack
more a
black pudding bursting
bloody bastes
the luminous ring
dances
lunar lines
across
the Green Man's playground
hiding wet
magenta
ribbons
and the scent is wafting
and the hirsute pursuer
pines for the
metallic tang
of a lone
lovely
languishing
in the green baize clearing
stupid morsel
needs eating

ravishing repast
Slurp slurp burp burp

Smell the meat my darling
now your
tastes are
refined
smell the meat my darling
now you're
a carnivorous
whore

Oh Alice! Put down That Seagull

Black humour. Based on an imagined retribution for a silly young woman from a flock of Seagulls, mad at her antics and attempts to steal their eggs. In order to capture the perfect "Insta" post!

Oh Alice! Put Down That Seagull

Sinister

On multi-coloured rocks
comedic seagulls
swipe
in swooping shifts
playing
a game of
chess
they nest and take turns
darting in and out
of their
cliff condominiums

Alice
A Nordic beauty
(if there was a contest)
wanted the
perfect Instagram
Swing-shot
bragging rights
how cool
her bleached head
looked
against beach and cliff

Reaching out
for Seagull eggs
the birds
suddenly
attack

Put down our young

Put down our young
they screech
all Alice can do
is reach for the ledge

Safely harnessed
she swings
like a teenage Ape
lunging grabbing at the Seagull's
hopes

The response is swift
razor sharp beaks
escape all intruders

Alice's eye
it's kebabbed and
ripped

Revenge is bloody
but just

The delicious damsel
stripped and pecked
carrion carved
hanging
till tourists rescue
too late to tell
her followers

#AlicesAmazingAdventures

23

Ode To A Chip

Wordplay and pastiche of Shakespeare's famous monologue in his 'Henry V' play.

Ode To A Chip
Funny

A Chip
A Chip
My Kingdom for
A Chip

Sorry Shakespeare-
It makes me salivate
those golden crusty morsels
on a plate
like golden embers
shiny glistening
basted pleasures
past remembering

Carbo-licious tasty treats
like fatty sticks
of dynamite

Dipped in mayo
for fancy Euros
best friends fish
for proper Brits

My Kingdom
I would certainly swap
for a chip-butty
from the chip shop

I, Plotter

*On a winter's day, looking out, daydreaming of revenge
on someone close who had betrayed me.*

Better to daydream violence than to carry it out!

I, Plotter
Revenge

I watch the
dreary damp
English gunship
weather
across the pane
as my breath
makes mean
'O's on the window
I plot
and seethe with
spleen

I resolve to
make a plan
plain enough
with peevishness
to punish

Buoyed by brevity
audacity in action
they would never
think I had the
gumption

The new me
leaves lip autographs
on slimy glass
forensics no doubt
will be grateful
that I blew a frozen kiss
to my darling dupe

The game has started
I know the rules
This time

Pageantry of Vanity

A comment about the ubiquitous "selfie" on social media. "Say Cheese!"

Pageantry of Vanity
Self-absorption

It's all about me me me
can't you see
no self-worth
without a selfie

Self-absorption
caring what others think
is a cheap exchange
for knowing
your true purpose
prostrating your
wares in exchange
for likes

Look At Me
Look At Me
watch my
blethering
watch my
bleating
and fakery

No time for a cuppa
a shoulder to rest on
a chinwag or two
just click the bell
and wait for the
pageantry

Laundered

Imagining the end of a relationship that once was good –
the clearing away of painful memory.

Laundered
Sadness

The rain
it cleanses all manner
of things
scouring the route
to redemption
and sorrow

like tears
they never fell
when I stood over your
still sullen shape

But now they do
like terrible trembling torrents
tormenting
washing the life we had
clean away

All stains are gone
you are erased
from our life

Like lines of laundered linens

A Civilised Move

Based on a true-life event during a holiday in Rhodes –
Watching the local Greek men playing Backgammon on
old board tables by the harbour wall.

A Civilized Move
Wry Observations

There's an art to life
play the game know the rules
then break some occasionally
but not all
it's draining to be in chaos
I've played
the game of Backgammon
with ancient Greeks who could
teach
us all a thing or two about living

Rhodes Island-
Mandraki harbour wall
round tables
men playing their games
they beat me obviously
I didn't know
their rules

But the game unfolded
like a Rubik's cube
fiendishly simple-clever

Dark shiny pebbles for eyes
boring into my Celtic reserve
tracking my every move
The ouzo left

greasy white trails on the tables
and the pebbles grew darker
with concentration

The drachma pile waxed and
waned
from my side mostly waned
I was distracted by
brighter
pebbles
the apprentice gods
chewing the fat with the
municipal fraternity

The Adonis that sat
opposite me
lifted my well trailed
glass
the gossamer imprint
of my lips
pressed to his

Focus ebbed away
the old pebbles
twinkled
the game plan worked
beware Greeks bearing gifts

Little Knots of Yellow

A childish thrill at seeing the twinkling lights of Bradford, in West Yorkshire, England spread across the hills and valleys coming home on dark winter nights.

Little Yellow Knots
Bradford, W. Yorkshire

The accelerator squeals
like an excited teenager
up the winding hill
all shrill grating and
gear crunching

Then the inward gasp
of childish awe
spread underneath
the tarmac ribbon crest
of a northern town sprawl
through misty drizzle
little knots of yellow lights
sparkling beams of
safety guiding
in the inky swathes
scrunched up bundles
of grey woolpack hills

Northern lights in
vaulted skies
through
pitiless winter washes

Welcome home to braids
of lantern sanctuary
welcome home
daughter
of the
shires

The Cult of Red Hair

I have loved Pre-Raphaelite paintings since my student days. I'd skip lectures and sneak out to the Birmingham Art Museum – It has one of the best collections in the world. I always admired those Titian haired lovelies and especially Lizzie Siddal. painter's muse and artist in her own right.

The Cult of Red Hair
Artist muse: Lizzie Siddal

I am a Pre-Raphaelite
enigma
with my flame red hair
and skin of alabaster

I am mistress

I am muse

I am bohemian and loud

I am personification of lust

I am sexually released

I am unforgettable

I am artiste

The Kiss of A Rancid Mouth

The horrible realisation that you're being used in a relationship, is disdainful and corrosive.

The Kiss of A Rancid Mouth
Disdain

I'll stand my turn
for a kiss
from the rancid mouth

It's in my mind
like a canker
beckoning me to
respond to its
sublime sulphurous
seep

Diabolo's cheer from
the deep swelling
depths
of fetid emotion

Rise up to
drown
the fiendish messages
I'm trying to mouth
soundlessly
to the man
who doesn't
weep
and
spits out
his disdain
endlessly

Eliminate

When you want to annihilate someone from your life...
just read this poem instead, it will keep you out of prison!

Eliminate

Anger

Like an acid attack
I want to burn off your
touch
scrub my skin with wire-wool
till I'm dripping with
blood
and taste the sweet tang of
repent

I hate you with a
passion
so terrifying
I spew
spit
piss
all the vile
bile burning
yellow
may you rot in a
canopy of cawl
from your first born
may it strangle
like a tourniquet
twist your purple pustules
till they split and
disgorge their
vituperous contents

You were made in
the Devil's smithy
white curls of poison
was the milk sustenance
from the

Jackal's teat
By all that is
Holy in my soul
I will slash
Burn
Bite
Stamp
anything
all of the above
to eliminate
the DNA of your derivation

Donegal Feast

I once had a lovely Irish boyfriend. On a trip home, he took me to a small cove off the west coast of Donegal and we spent a happy afternoon plundering the biggest mussels I've ever seen!

Donegal Feast
Irish memory

Mud as black as pitch
sucking between my toes
its unctuous texture
slippery and sensual

All of this
on a perfect Irish day
no rain to obscure
nature's bounty
revealed at low tide

Mussels as big as a baby's fist
delicious fare from
dangerous tides
ready to swipe away
my greedy plundering

Sticky squelching slime
trapping feet
in sharp rocks
blessed landscape
ripening and devouring
my hunger

Perspiration rising
my haul is landed

A fire
A pot
A knife
Neptune's vittles
satisfy my salty chase
pilgrim thief-
I slip into happy
alliance with my ancient
Celtic ancestors

My heritage fused
with the pearl of
mussel shell paths

The Name Game – Fun On the Tongue

As the title suggests, just a fun tongue-twister. It's why we love nursery rhymes. Nonsense but pleasing to the ear!

The Name Game – Fun On The Tongue

Fun Tongue-twister

What's in a name

If Carolina wears a carabiner
And Charlotta
travels far
In her car

Will Phillip pass
the stirrups
and
Matt
his hat

Why does Wycliffe
need his handcuff
and Gracie
need a lift

Will that be
too much for
Smithy if
Sally eats the
pith

Can Heather find
the feather
in her pillow
for
little Willow

What's in a name
by evidence
no substance
but absurd
rest assured

Untethered

Learning to mellow out with age when a partner pushes all your buttons!

Untethered
Anger Mellowed

Strewn socks
litter the stairwell
floating down
in woolly
vollies

It's not a
sexual awakening

I throw the
fusillade of socks
instead of bricks
they lay
untethered
from my feet
my ire
is a slaughter of footwear
salvos
instead of shrapnel
tearing your body

A soft slow motion
attack
of fleecy artillery

The point is made

A scattering of
stirred sentiment
on the stairs
better mismatched
socks
than spilt
blood

Ours Is The Fury

A comment about being outraged by terrorism in all its forms.

Ours is The Fury
Fury

My unsheathed sword is
dulled
I smile slowly
I'm a survivor

I've wrought woeful
horror
on unsuspecting neighbour
I smile cruelly
I'm a lover

If I was the
Knight-in-armour
with battles brought
before Kings
the rose-tint of history
would excuse these things

But I'm not

I'm a modern barbarian
and ours is the fury
that shall not speak its name
for the want of salvation

Metamorphic

Remembering significant places in my life.

I once embarrassed my daughter in front of her teenage friends by announcing on a visit to the coast, "Oh look, that's where you were conceived!"

She's never really forgiven me for being nicknamed "Rock Girl" after that!

Metamorphic
British landscape: Hunstanton

As landscapes go
it's not dramatic
no high planes drama
no fragmented paving stones
the cliffs are banded
like wrapped candy-cane

Not even a lighthouse
to relieve the endless
horizon

It has a timeless sense
of space
I could be a Victorian
a genteel stroller
or rockers' moll
enjoying an ice cream

I enjoy sitting
on a gluteus shaped
dip of rock
on the shoreline
A noteworthy place
in my heart
the place of my daughter's
genesis

She was formed during
the soft ebbing and
swoosh of sea
on seashore
I return and sit
still and somnolent
oftentimes to think
and record the
metamorphic changes
in my life
mirroring
my place of healing
my bottom shaped
touchstone

Thoughts From Lancelot du Lac

This is from a series of poems I wrote based on Arthurian legends. This one imagines a knight character from the imaginary 'Camelot'. Lancelot seemed very in-love with himself!

Thoughts from Lancelot du Lac
Narcissism

I'm supposed to be the FIRST
knight
you know
the gallant heroic gritty one
of the round-table boys club

I want to sit by Guinevere
stroke her moistness
she really needs it
what does it matter that
Arthur isn't here
bit inconvenient
when I want to shag his queen

I'm handy with my sword
all the women agree my
blade is thick and strong
and tempered for performance

These medieval girl-women
so grateful
for a good servicing
when their husbands are
fighting holy wars
can't stand the pretend
screaming on their
Prima Nocta though-
It hurts so good girls
I'm doing you a big throbbing
favour
for your first fumbling
now Guinevere is
whining and crying
in her nunnery
she needs some maintenance
I'll pay her a visit for a
special Knightly night

I love playing the hero
such a great role

UnMothered

A much-loved daughter leaving home to go off to University. The utter wrench of a grieving "empty-nester" mother.

UnMothered
Loss

Run
abandon her
flee the binding cord
you toss aside the
Mother-love
like last years
tatty ragdoll
blithely embracing
your shiny new northern life

Insouciant shrug

What does it matter
that your
mother is
crushed
life previously unravelling
with you as the leading
player
dissolving like wet celluloid

Her memories merge
like one huge
sob
and yet this irrigation
will provide a
fecundity
of new adventures
she's so infuriated
inactive
and sacked
Her grief is
sodden and bloated
begging to be
drowned
Uncoupled Unchilded
Unmothered

My Moat of Dust

Remembering my lovely Dad. RIP Ray Williams.

My Moat of Dust
Loss

I have a direct line
to the Universe
he calls me daily
in my head

You showed me that
in our cosmic
communications
I am unique
I know my value

One can look
at cooling cinder
in awe
of its once brilliance
the way I now look
at your kinder face
in my remembrance

Diamonds to dust
our moat
can cross
to the only place
where our love
exists
forever

Punching Paint

I watched a documentary about artists in New York, throwing paint at one another at an Art installation. Reminded me of several religious festivals around the world that do this...fun & messy!

Punching Paint
Whimsical

A school of performing art-
punching paint from
paintbrush limbs

Spraying speckled heliotrope
across the gallery space
a fist of vermillion
POW
a gloved chartreuse
CRACK
azure haze of tinctures
THUMP

Round one to freedom
of expression
round two outdoor
canvass
round three to
brutal artisan

Drawing crowds of
rainbow creatives
grappling their flaws
punching out their
pigments

Purple Freedom

Meditating and sitting still enough to listen to those messages only we can hear.

Purple Freedom

Fate

In my head my pretty head
I am diminished
in my eyes my pretty eyes
I am clairvoyant

I see purple
or a mix
of red and blue

The point is my pretty point is
my auric hues confuse

So goodbye my head
my eyes
my sentinel
to the other me

I see purple
it sounds like silence
it feels like thread

I pull the twine sublime
connection
to my head
to my Source

I am removed
of course
I am free
my conscious
IS
me

Khaki Rainbows

Observations, waiting by a quayside for the fishing boats from Shetland to cross to mainland Scotland. It was Winter. The weather was wild!

Khaki Rainbows
Fishing boats from Shetland

Thunderous sprays of khaki
rainbows
smeared the view today
the unremitting gloom
of Shetland skies scurried
over once Viking island rooms

No romance bestowed
from Nordic-like skies
no ancient ruins
bestowing benign chance

The pig-squeal of wipers
like balloons
squashed on silica windscreens
waves crashing through the
drear dry-dock
A caught chain crusting
with ferrous markings
like a ghost snake
wrapped around
the fish-filters pots

Waiting valiantly quayside
the fishing boats bobbing
carrying their human cargo
umbilically to Scottish
shores

Closer to Stavanger than
London
these daily commutes challenge
in winters woeful wrath

Remember To Forget Me

Not wanting to stay friends after a relationship breakdown.
Well, why would you?

Remember to Forget Me
Loss

You MUST forget me as

To do otherwise
Is to
tear
wrench
torture
what's left
of me

I'm left on promenades
walking in straight lines
but
not reaching my
destination
just jutting out in
rough seas

I float on
firm footing
over boiling cauldrons
but we all know
the soup
is now spoilt

I can bear all
if you are
bleached and
whitened
out of
my life

Remember to forget me
Who are
You?

Moonlight Gossamer

Saying goodbye to a loved one. Imagining a beautiful moth carrying a message of love to the Moon.

Moonlight Gossamer

Loss

Our love is like
moonlight gossamer
ethereal
beautiful
like a silver moth
in flight

The shape of them
a silver ship
a lovely thing to
carry
our dreams and hopes
to Heaven
with so delicate
a thread
the argent arrows
of the night
throw silver tips
into ice-glass
shards of gleam

A lone moth
breaks free
flutters to earth
one final kiss
a wisp
woven
into
goodbye
goodbye
goodbye

Possibilities

Looking at your child – they are a work in progress. A reflection of ourselves can be uncomfortable sometimes.

Possibilities

Love

My daughter sits at the table
I know how she tilts her head
like mine
and she's always able
to mimic
my comedy foibles

I wonder
as I gaze
on her wistful face how
she will find
herself
without her co-pilot

I will long
For her adventures
to start
my child-woman
as she stumbles
into her life

My daughter
is me
but with possibilities
don't you see?

Hot Ginger

Love messing around with rhyme and assonance.

No great insight here, just "Word Foolery"

Hot Ginger
Wordplay

It's in the tingle
of a
hot ginger
toddy
that turns me on
when my body
needs some
fire

Or

It's in the quiver
of a
hot ginger
'body'
that turns me on
when my figure
needs some
fire

Curvy Edge

There comes a time when we all feel a bit "past it". Decided to go for a striking hair dye transformation. Turned heads, as it was so shocking!

Curvy Edge
Ageing

Too plump
to be seen like those
rock-chick Chrissy's

I look in the mirror
more like
sweet-shop rock
and prissy

Taking a stand
to pimp the
crowning glory
I finally found
the missing edge
it was no ordinary
sensible silver

Shimmering rainbows
streaking through
the titanium mane
tossing my
iridescent hues
I dress my hair
turning heads

Suddenly
I'm curvy-cool
edgy

I'll Read Your Smile

Understanding love as it plays out and develops in relationships.

I'll Read Your Smile

Romance

I read your smile
nothing lovelier to me
than the gap between
nose and chin

It lights you up
the bright handsome
version
with good teeth
I noticed your smile
before the
shoulders
head
hair
beguiling eyes

Others notice
this male beauty too
I used to fret
that smile
wasn't

exclusive
But you return
all smiles
all manly
all delicious
like plump apple crisp

I read your smile
I become avaricious
for the sweet juice kiss

I read your smile
it told me
the whole truth
you love MY smile
and kiss the nectar first

Driftwood

Rescuing a damaged soulmate; being someone's safe harbour.

Driftwood
Finding love

In my quiet contemplations
I see your face
it floats into my mind
abstract driftwood
washing up on my shoreline

In needs a home
a calm scene
in my hands
it's wondrous art
let it have a place
at my hearth
a decorous piece
to be admired

The woodgrain flows
down
to earth
my soul
the forgotten traces
made null
by erosion

You are beautiful
my rescued art
my future story
salvaged from the
timber
wreckage of your life

I Change My Men Like I Change my Socks

The revolving door of men in and out of my life during my 30's was noted by my family. I shut them up by eventually settling down with a decent chap!

I Change My Men Like I Change My Socks
Fate

I change my men
like I change my socks

-or so my mother fears-

She's always slightly
appalled
amused even
that I'm good
at getting men
but distrustful
at the thought of me
keeping them

I lie to myself
it's variety I need

NO

I'm as conventional
as the next woman
traditional to the core
I want to wear
his and hers socks
keep them in
our sock drawer
forever

Shiver Down The Glass

The utter shock of being replaced in a relationship, smashing your self-worth to smithereens.

Shiver Down The Glass
Being replaced

Small mean 'O' of mouth
on frosted glass between us
the ambient temperature
dropped to zero
after you told me
you were leaving

What I really want to do
Is shiver down that glass
into razor shards
and cut you
out of my life
I want to
throw the rocks
you keep by the bolted door
for scaring off the old crows
but you think I'm one of
that murdering bunch now
so I resist

I'll scare off the human form
left like gauze on the cold pane
that reflection of you
the earlier version I loved
now that youth has cracked
into senility
the reflection needs to be
annihilated
and erased from my antique eyes
leaving me free
to construct new planes
placed at different angles
to capture the dying light

Now England

A vivid, nostalgic memory of being homesick for England after arriving in Warsaw, Poland. Didn't know the language or have a soul to talk to.

Now England
Emigres Memory in Poland

Vaughn Williams'
'Lark Ascending' playing softly
triggering my emigre
memory

Sitting by the hotel window
in Warsaw
a secondment overseas
to paint pictures
of English culture
using my mother tongue
I'm moved with the vision
of verdant fields, panoramic skies
and Lincolnshire cornfields
contrasting
with the soft drubbing
of snow blanketing the
hard grey monuments along the
'Nowy Swiat'
Tears stream down

powdered cheeks
like melted snow through
trickling trails
at the remembering

Sentimental yearning
for my home
my England
a place away from cities
my soul ascends into
azure skies
and lessens the ache

Shimmer

Ageing gracefully...or not!

Shimmer
Ageing gracefully

The ordinariness of the day
contrasted with the
epiphany
that followed

Another tedious chore-
the packet of false
hirsute promises
stayed on the
bathroom floor

Was led to believe
youth captured
now held ransom
to self-fulfilling prophecy
of guessing one's age

The beauty peddlers
and female pardoners
convinced us
with trickery
that grey hues
were meant only
for the downhill-don't-care
brigades

Freedom
feels like softly silken ropes
shimmering
with steel glints
tumbling with crowning
argentum glory

Arid

For those feeling rejected and past their "sell-by-date".

Arid
Ageing

My femininity is going to waste
every year that passes
I'm withering inside
like a neglected cactus
nurture my elementals
affection
comfort
loyalty
my cactus needs more than water
I've absorbed
too much toxic rain
rotting my roots
I need to draw fresh moisture
I need a new oasis

All is arid
dry
desiccated
I hanker for
irrigation
to be sprinkled and refreshed

My late blooms
can still be
valiant
spectacular and
magnificent

Sweetheart Bastards

Finding love when you're middle-aged is hard work. Enough said!

Sweetheart Bastards
Disappointment

If my pussy could talk
it would want hours of
conversation
with a larger than life
character

Preparing to host
an event
would include
trimming foliage
around the grounds
washing down surfaces
clearing debris
the ambiance would
flow for chatting

My pussy could listen
For hours
in a deep
meaningful connection
but the
sweetheart bastards
just want a quick
gossip

The Swagger of A Woman Past Midnight

It's considered taboo to discuss mature women's sexual urges...well, I just did!

The Swagger of A Woman Past Midnight
Maturity

Some like travel & wine
big lungfuls of space
to breathe
like biting on oxygen
and hitting a six

Some get their swag on
opening windows
gulping in the Universe
eating raw and meditating

Food drink and sex
meat wine and orgasms

The clock chimes midnight
the woman in me pulses
sleepy veins
surge awake

I hit a six
I sleep the unfathomable
sleep of a buddha
at one with tranquillity
until the summer light
filters urgency
and the swagger
of a woman
past the midday
of her life

Antique Mustard

Getting down and dirty with the paint charts at home!

Antique Mustard
Hot sex

Antique Mustard
is a hot colour
with real heat
designers
wash it all over walls
for impact

I never really liked it
but the colourist
told me it was
energising
only said it was
divine
to grab your
undivided attention
so you'd be inclined
to behave
like a rampant
dog

The pre-paint sex
was splashed
on the walls
mingled with the
energetic secretions

It's a primitive pleasure
to look at walls
and secretly
want to
sniff
them

Crescendo

Passionate embraces with a partner outside in nature.

Crescendo
Passion

We walk to the edge of the cliff
the wind blows and makes
sweeping darts across my face
the sting and slap of wet hair
beating out natures force
rhythmically

Pulse pulse rise rise

I feel giddy looking over the edge
seeing the white combs
gathering a pace and hitting
their fury over granite crags

Smash smash boom boom

Your hand finds mine and
tugs me close your mouth
smothers
all reproof – I feel the surge
succumbing to delicious delirium

Swell swell throb throb

As you lift my face to yours
sweeping my buffeted hair
out of my eyes
you kiss wax-like skin
and blooms of carmine hue
burst forth driving your
Animation

Pulse pulse rise rise

Screaming shorelines slip
into auditory
WHOA

Thundering combing
squealing rush

It powers your ardour
and the surrounding wrath
is mirrored in our lust

Pound pound crash crash

Tearing rages stinging
whips of hair
rising flush and
moistened fresh
CRESCENDO
is drowned
by the breaking ocean

Dying

On

Its

M o m e n t u m

95

Bad Hair Days

Don't you just love it when you meet someone staggering, and you look like you've been pulled through a hedge backwards? Well, I imagined a scenario where both parties looked shocked!

Bad Hair Days
Fate

Wind howls in pain
the door swings
I'm caught in
tubes
of aerodynamic slings

Hair in rods
devoid of style
I chanced upon
the dream man

Pushing past like timetabled
trains
the man-made vacuum
sucks exchanged
hair gelled
sympathy

Passing through the wind tunnel
experiment
a knowing glance
did register

He recognises
good hair when he
sees his
mirror image

I hold my breath in
anticipation
He holds the door

His fate is sealed

Serendipity

Fate - don't knock it. It's been responsible for some real twists and turns in my life. Serendipity keeps life interesting!

Serendipity
Fate

Fate's friend
chance to
steer
life's
destiny

Come to me
in strange times
out of the blue

It might be
round the
corner

If it's meant
to be
it will
be
serendipity

PART 2
The Journal Section

If you've never journaled before it might be helpful to understand how journaling can help you express and develop your thoughts and emotions.

Journals are individual pieces of writing and expressions of personal growth, interests, opinions and observations about your life. They are usually private which can allow you to write honestly and to pour your emotions out onto the page.

Two aspects are important to bear in mind. While this form of writing is very 'free' and not in chronological order like a diary, for ease of readability, write paragraphs and organise your thoughts with themes or dates. This is where the more creative amongst you can really go to town with your coloured pens and highlighters to demarcate different aspects of your writing.

Those who like to blog will have a head start but even those that do it regularly will find that the *physical* act of writing words on a page seems to be more powerful. It allows your *persona, your individual voice,* to come out.

Do you have a certain voice in life but another in your head? For example, in my everyday life, my tone is upbeat and witty. However, when I write, I can mine a deep well of dark dystopian thoughts!

Do you have a little script you tell yourself whenever you have to make decisions about your future?

What's your most vivid or recurring dream? Do you have experiences in life that keep repeating? What's the hardest lesson in life you've had to learn?

These questions could stimulate your mind to explore your internal thoughts. Negative thoughts can be explored in safety, they are valid as a marker to review and update or to take action on.

You have the power within you to answer your internal dialogue!

Shadow Time

The Journal Section

The Journal Section

Shadow Time

The Journal Section

Shadow Time

Shadow Time

Shadow Time

The Journal Section

Shadow Time

Shadow Time

Shadow Time

The Journal Section

Shadow Time

Shadow Time

Shadow Time

The Journal Section

Shadow Time

Shadow Time

Shadow Time

Shadow Time

The Journal Section

Shadow Time

The Journal Section

Shadow Time

The Journal Section

Shadow Time

The Journal Section

Shadow Time

Shadow Time

The Journal Section

Shadow Time

The Journal Section

Shadow Time

The Journal Section

Shadow Time

The Journal Section

Shadow Time

The Journal Section

Shadow Time

The Journal Section

Shadow Time

Shadow Time

The Journal Section

The Journal Section

Shadow Time

The Journal Section

CONCLUSION

I do feel journaling is a more fashionable way of documenting life events and emotions. It seems to be quite the accepted practice for noting gratitude and finding clarity for personal actions.

I wish I'd thought of journaling as a way of self-care years ago when I was going through some tough times in my life.

One of the worst episodes was when I emigrated to America back in the 1990's. I had married an American teacher of History. We had met by chance whilst we were both on International teaching posts, teaching TEFL (Teaching English As a Foreign Language) in Poland.

We had the most romantic and passionate romance in Warsaw. It was the perfect 'holiday' romance; we were both like fish-out-of-water, we had suspended our domestic arrangements to do the teaching contracts and were caught up in the history and glamour of the Polish Capital.

Before Poland joined the EU, you had to obtain a visa to remain in the country. As luck would have it, 18 months into our relationship, we discovered our visas would run out within a month of each other. We had to make some pretty big decisions. We had to decide if we wanted to continue our relationship or part as loving friends.

We decided to marry. It was the only way we could remain together in a close relationship and return to either America or the UK. Both immigration processes were arduous. Both required sacrifice.

Fatefully, I decided to burn my bridges; uproot my 6-year-old daughter, marry my American history teacher and emigrate to his family home in a small, rural community in Massachusetts.

The internet was in its infancy and my only real catch-up with the UK was through my weekly dial-up session online with AOL. My daughter would "see" her grandparents and chatter about all things she loved about the American way of life - playing softball, cheerleading, fire pit BBQ's in our large top paddock with our horses, snow-angels and pancake stacks for breakfast from IHOP with enough maple syrup to keep the dentist busy for years.

It was in effect, a forerunner of the Zoom experience we have today – except it was sporadic and made me feel very dispirited after seeing close family. I felt like I had to remain chatty and upbeat after dragging their beloved grandchild thousands of miles across the Atlantic.

The reality was very different. I was very lonely. It had been an utter culture shock arriving in the US after spending time in Eastern Europe. Even though, as a Brit, I was universally liked as soon as they heard a British accent, I knew I'd made a mistake within the first year of my marriage.

The crushing realisation I'd made a real error of judgement came one night when my husband came home completely stoned out of his head on drugs. Then hit me when I had the nerve to question him about it. It came completely out of the blue. The shock and bruising receded over a period of time with my husband saying it would never happen again; he was under so much pressure with work. He was indeed extra loving for a few weeks. I tried to logically file it away into "it's a one-off" file in my head.

The crushing loneliness of being an immigrant in a strange country with a different culture and a sinking feeling that my husband appeared to act like a completely different person to the man I'd met 2 years previously out in Warsaw.

I cried many times when driving alone in my car, calling out to my mum. I really missed my family and just wanted to tell them I was miserable. But I had a responsibility to my little girl who was blissfully unaware of the growing tensions and absolutely loved her new life in America.

I did eventually screw up my courage a couple of years later and returned to the UK with my daughter, but I literally came away with nothing. I had to restart my life again on my own with my little girl and claw my way back to stability and happiness.

If I had established the habit of writing my feelings down in a daily journal, I would have decompressed my emotions of utter fury and frustration. I would have learned how to cope with the altered reality of living as an immigrant and having to deal with petty bureaucrats at immigration control in Boston, MA. It may not have sown the seeds of destruction within my marriage.

So, journaling can be a powerful self-care tool to evoke mindfulness and to keep you present in the flow of positive creativity. Journaling, the process of connecting pen to paper, stimulates the hand-to-eye coordination in the brain. It triggers regulation of emotions- to produce a greater sense of confidence and self-identity.

If for no other reason than to keep your chaotic 'soup' of floating ideas spinning out of control in your mind, ramping up your potential anxiety – I urge you to journal.

Pick it up. Open it up. Read the poems. Skip past those you don't quite connect with, linger over the ones you do like and let the words say something to you.

At the very least, feast your eyes upon the beautiful illustrations my friend and fine artist Sally Brown has produced; her designs are sought after and have given life to my words.

I knew I wanted to use the word 'Shadow' with 'Time' in my title. Writing is such a contemplative activity, the 'Shadow Time' is time apart from family and daily demands.

I wanted to use an image that supported my whole ethos about 'Shadow Time'.

The image of a Snow Leopard literally popped into my head when I was daydreaming in my home office one day. It was a fleeting thought that lodged into the tiny crevices of my mind in an instant. My soul just recognised it, I had goosebumps when I heard it in my head. I had an innate gut-feeling that it was right for this project.

I quickly logged onto the internet to research the characteristics of a Snow Leopard: Solitary. Powerful. Courageous. That was it! I had found the perfect animal spirit totem to support my work.

Writing has awakened a latent vein of creativity in me – I now put time aside to channel my writing during my working week now. I absolutely love doing it. It's my joyful, quiet time.

Let this be YOUR creative 'Shadow Time' and let the Snow Leopard guide your words.

I hope you're well on your way to developing your 'voice' in your writing.

What aspects of writing did you enjoy?

Have you found a favourite time to write?

"There's a trick to the graceful exit – it begins with the vision to recognise when a job, a relationship or life stage is over – and let it go. It means leaving what's over without denying its validity or its importance in our lives. It involves a sense of future, a belief that every exit line is an entity, that we are moving up, rather than out".

- Ellen Goodman

"Build your life on your dreams, because dreams never have bad endings."

-M F Moonzajer

ACKNOWLEDGEMENTS

Firstly, my lovely husband, Gary has borne the brunt of my ire with my laptop. It used to be my daughter Rachel's turn to catch the frustrations with all things technical – now the baton has firmly passed to Gary. Steadfast and calm with magic powers of coaxing my old MacBook Air to do all the things I imagined it should do.

Many thanks darling, I apologise for being grumpy with you sometimes during its execution. You know I love you to the Moon and back.

My dear friends, Femke, Amanda and Helen are beautiful, savvy professional businesswomen. They have collectively written my endorsement and have all followed my journey to become a writer with interest and encouragement. The "Secret Squirrel Club" has provided fun, giggles and virtual shoulders to cry on.

Sally Brown; a friend and talented illustrator is such a creative powerhouse. Her stunning drawings have supported my words and elevated this journal to a thing of beauty. I'm so grateful to you Sally. Clare Froggatt from 'Make A Brew'- Her graphic design of the front cover made me gasp when I saw the first draft. She'd taken my sketchy ideas about its layout and manifested an eye-catching cover. Thanks Clare.

Emily Gowor; A bright, sparkly, inspiring author and publisher deserves special thanks for supporting my efforts and providing sage advice about taking action with this creative project. Plus, the encouragement from her team at Gowor International Publishing. They have truly helped me find my voice and purpose as a poet and fledgling author.

ABOUT THE AUTHOR

Ellie LaCrosse is a Poet and a Communicator.

She is also a mentor to several female business owners and creator of a successful networking group called *The Cashmere Club*. Where she helps to raise funds for her chosen female health charity: Endometriosis UK.

Entrepreneurial in spirit, this is her first poetry anthology journal and her entry as a writer and author.

Ellie divides her time by supporting and developing her many business interests, exploring her writing skills, supporting female business owners and indulging her passion for interior design. She also produces content with her regular podcast *(Ellie-LaCrosse)/ Little Red Typewriter on Spotify,* where she invites established writers to chat to her audience about what motivated them to become a writer.

To book Ellie for a Keynote Presentation or Speaking Engagement:

Ellie@littleredtypewriter.com

+44 07747 057 028

Lightning Source UK Ltd.
Milton Keynes UK
UKHW050915160122
397202UK00005B/43

9 781739 835606